Mindful Beyond

MINDFUL BEYOND

POEMS AND MEDITATIONS OF GOD'S MASTERPIECES

ABBIE HAYDEN HUTH

Charleston, SC
www.PalmettoPublishing.com

Mindful Beyond
Copyright © 2022 by Abbie Hayden Huth

First Edition

Hardcover ISBN: 978-1-68515-897-2
Paperback ISBN: 978-1-68515-898-9

TABLE OF CONTENTS

MINDFUL moments

What are the moments
that make you feel small?
The moments that take your breath
and gently force you to pause in awe?

The promise of a new day
in the colors of the morning skies?
The joy of new life
in those first newborn cries?

Maybe the view of blue skies and open fields
stretched for miles and miles?
Or the quietness in the forest
bringing peace seemingly erasing all your trials?

Is it the majestic view from the mountaintop,
with endless beauty expanding far below?
Or the glistening of sunlight
on the water or freshly fallen snow?

Is it the vastness of the sea
you admire walking along the coast?
Or is it the radiance of a sunset
that humbles you the most?

Be mindful of these moments,
moments generously given by our Creator,
The moments our soul is reminded
we are all a part of something much greater.

Be mindful of these moments
that put your heart at ease.
Find rest in knowing,
You are God's most cherished masterpiece.

Be mindful of these moments,
beyond what your mind can comprehend
These moments created to bring unspeakable joy,
by the One who loves you with no end.

He performs wonders that cannot be fathomed,
miracles that cannot be counted.
  - Job 5:9 NIV -

The steadfast love of the Lord never ceases, his mercies
never come to an end; they are new every morning;
great is your faithfulness.
-Lamentations 3: 22-23 ESV

In the morning when you rise,
you notice so does the sun.
You find hope in the skies
as they softly declare, "a new day has begun!"

Bright colors spread far and wide,
proving the Master Artist never left our side.
Each morning He reveals a new masterpiece
to remind of His mercies that never cease.

The sun peeks up over the hills
surrounded by colors that thrill.
In confidence, you arise
knowing you too, are created by the painter of the skies.

Pink, orange, and brushstrokes of purple too,
the colors proclaim the start of a fresh new day
created with a purpose just for you,
So rise up and let's get on your way!

AFFIRMATION:

I rise with the sun. I have a unique purpose painted just for me today. The God who paints the skies in the mornings, also knows every detail about me. Thank you God, for the beautiful promise of a new day.

I lift my eyes to the mountains.
Where does my help come from?
My help comes from the Lord,
maker of heaven and earth.
Psalm 121:1-2, NIV

MIGHTY mountain

Mighty and strong,
I stand like a mountain that cannot be moved.
High above all creation,
the mountain overlooks life all abounding.
Grassy fields waving below,
and a colorful sky boasting behind,
still the mountain stands in beauty of its own.
Confident and bold,
brave and fierce,
refusing to be shaken,
prepared to conquer whatever comes my way.
With the same might as a mountain,
in full assurance I climb,
believing I can do all things
in this strength beyond my own.

Affirmation:

I am mighty. I am strong. I am confident and bold. I am brave and beautiful. I will not be moved or shaken. I can do all things. I can conquer whatever comes my way with strength that is already inside of me.

Look at the lilies and how they grow. They don't
work or make their clothing, yet Solomon in all his
glory was not dressed as beautifully as they are.
    And if God cares so wonderfully for flowers that
are here today and thrown into the fire tomorrow,
        he will certainly care for you.

            — Luke 12:27-28 NLT

LOVED
as the
wildflowers

Softest, green grass under my feet,
bluest open skies far above.
The smell of the wildflowers extra sweet
in the meadow that whispers, "you are enough".

All across the field, the wildflowers grow.
No matter where they are placed they know
to rise up together and live life beautifully.
To accept where they are and to just be.

Like a wildflower, you can live free,
boldly blooming into who you were created to be.
You are unique and loved just as you are,
you are more than enough, by far.

Affirmation:

*I breathe in. I breathe out. I just be.
I am enough. Right where I am now.
No matter where I am or what I'm
faced with, I am free to just be.
I am growing even here.
I am unique and bring my
own beauty to the world.
I am loved as a wildflower.*

You rule the raging of the sea;
when its waves rise, you still them.
psalm 89:9, ESV

Breathe in, feel your heart rise like an ocean wave.
Breathe out, let your worries roll to the shore.
Breathe in the warm sun rays on your face,
Breathe out, let your toes sink in the cool sand.
Breathe in, silence.
Breathe out, the sound of smooth crashing waves.

The ocean waves are constant,
their rhythm repeats all day and all through the night.
The One who directs the waves
is also gently guiding you and me.
The rhythm of His faithfulness never ends.

Even when the winds get rough
the waves are always pulled back to shore.
Just as He stills the raging seas
He calms and carries us too.

Breathe in. Be still.
Breathe out. Be still.
Let Him embrace you safely back to shore.

Affirmation:

I am safe. I rise and I fall and I go with the flow. I am guided and calmed by the Ruler of the seas. Smooth or stormy seas, I am carried by His constant faithfulness. The rhythms of faithfulness pull me back to shore.

Be still, and know that I am God.
Psalm 46:10 ESV

EMBRACED BY
Shades of green

A place to listen and grow,
to be still and know.
Just as the trees stand bold and strong,
in the forest, I know I am right where I belong.

In the forest I feel free,
safely covered by a secure oak tree.
In the quietness I hear nothing but the wind
singing a soft song that only my heart can comprehend.

It whispers, "you are not alone"
as the leaves on the trees are softly blown.
Dancing with the gentle breeze
the leaves echo songs of peace.

Rays of golden light pierce a warm glow
and in the radiant stillness I know,
even at the times I don't understand,
I am covered by the One who holds a greater plan.

Affirmation:

I am free. I am a work of art, just as the forest is painted in every shade of green. I am gentle like the wind and strong and secure like the oak tree. In the quietness, I am not alone. I am surrounded and embraced by the golden light, glowing on all the forest trees. I am safe. In God, I find peace and security.

And the peace of God, which surpasses
all understanding, will guard your hearts
and your minds in Christ Jesus.
- Philippians 4:7

PAPA'S pond

Sitting at the edge of the dock
with my feet hovering just above the water.
On the clear pond, I see a reflection.
A reflection of the trees and a reflection of me.

The water reflects the thought, "you are alive".
Alive, just as the surrounding trees.
Shimmers of sunlight come alive
as they glisten and dance across the glassy pond.

The sounds of leaves shaking on the edge of their branches,
whispering, "you are exactly where you are meant to be",
as they hang on tightly
through the final days of autumn.

One rosy red leaf floats under my feet,
carried by the water's ripples and drifting of the wind.
Watching the red leaf pass by, I feel the crisp air
as the November sunshine warms my rosy cheeks.

The breeze reminds me once again, "I am alive".
The red leaf reminds me, I go with the flow and I let go.
I allow myself to change with the season.
I focus and find joy in each moment, trying not to let each day drift on by.
When the days get busy and start passing too quickly,
I come back to Papa's pond
to be still, to feel alive again.

Affirmation:

I feel the warmth of the sun of my face. The cool breeze on my skin. I am alive. I see my reflection, reminding me I am loved and beautiful and made for a purpose. I let go like the autumn leaves. I allow change and give myself grace. I embrace seasons of rest. I float like the leaves and go with the flow. I come to my Father to find peace and to find rest.

The heavens declare the glory of God,
and the sky above proclaims
his handiwork.
psalm 19:1, ESV

Radiant Hope

At the end of a long day
always remember to look up.
In the evening sky
there may be a message painted just for you.
Shades of orange and pink that can't be matched
quickly fading to magenta, violet, and darker night blue.
The Artist delights in His work
leaving a radiant note of redeeming love.
The skies are His canvas
promising us He is always near.
His paintbrush boasts of His goodness
as it fills the open sky with unimaginable hues.
Another day is coming to an end,
but look up and delight in Him,
see the masterpiece expectantly proclaiming
a bright new hope for tomorrow.

Affirmation:

*I am a masterpiece, created by the painter
of the skies. As He delights in His art in
the sky, even more so He delights in me.
The Master Artist has a unique beautiful
plan for my life. The setting sun leaves
a bright new hope for my tomorrow.*

He determines the number of the stars;
he gives to all of them their names.
Great is our Lord, and abundant in power;
his understanding is beyond measure.

psalm 147:4-5, ESV

Stillness
UNDER THE
STARS

I breathe in and close my eyes
as I lift my face to the starry skies.
I breathe out and feel so small
under a vast sky filled with wonder and awe.

Trillions of stars shining above
an entire universe exclaiming God's love.
He counts each star and calls them by name,
isn't it amazing He created and loves us the same?

My eyes see nothing but the stars so far away.
My heart feels calm as I come to the end of another day.
My body feels stillness and light
as I close my eyes and look up to whisper, "good night".

Affirmation:

As I go to bed tonight, I rest in knowing I am cherished and loved. I am a masterpiece created by the God of the entire universe. He designed millions of galaxies far above, yet also calls me His beloved. Even when my mind cannot ever understand the vastness of this love, I go to sleep knowing I am among the stars as a masterpiece of God. I shine with a unique purpose. I am chosen and set apart. I am loved beyond what I can imagine.

When I look at your heavens, the work of your fingers,
the moon and the stars, which you have set in place,
what is man that you are mindful of him, and the
son of man that you care for him?
—Psalm 8:3-4 ESV

the details

Slow down and take notice,
God is in the details.
Graciously He shows us,
both in the small and in the big-He never fails.

He is glistening on the morning dew,
in the midst of making all things new.
He's in the delicate petals of a daisy,
while still boldly working in ways we cannot see.

He designed every snowflake,
each and every one unique.
And when swirling blizzards of life may come,
He is still our strength when we are weak.

He is magnificent in the deep storm clouds,
then boasting in the hopeful hues of a rainbow.
He whispers through the cool summer breeze,
while still fighting battles before we even know.

He draws the veins on every leaf,
while also carefully crafting the veins to our heart.
Every pattern and design made on purpose,
proving He's had a special plan from the very start.

He knows the number of hairs on our heads,
and still names the stars from beginning to end.
He holds the whole world in nail scarred hands,
yet even one broken heart He is able to mend.

God is in the details,
both the big and the small.
Slow down and take notice,
He is there with us through it all.

I will remember the deeds of the LORD;
yes, I will remember your wonders of old.
I will ponder all your work, and
meditate on your mighty deeds.

         –psalm 77:11-12 ESV